W9-AYO-469

Date: 10/18/11

571 .6 SHE
Sherman, Josepha.
How do we know the nature
of the cell /

Great Scientific
Questions and the
Scientists Who
Answered Them™

HOW DO WE KNOW

THE NATURE
OF THE CELL

JOSEPHA SHERMAN

Great Scientific
Questions and the
Scientists Who
Answered Them™

HOW DO WE KNOW
THE NATURE
OF THE CELL

THE ROSEN PUBLISHING GROUP, INC.
NEW YORK

Published in 2005 by The Rosen Publishing Group, Inc.
29 East 21st Street, New York, NY 10010

Copyright © 2005 by The Rosen Publishing Group, Inc.

First Edition

Library of Congress Cataloging-in-Publication Data

Sherman, Josepha.
How do we know the nature of the cell/by Josepha Sherman.
    p. cm. —Great scientific questions and the scientists who
    answered them)
Summary: Reviews discoveries that led to mankind's understanding
that the cell is the fundamental unit of living material in all organisms,
and how that understanding has impacted the science of biology.
Includes bibliographical references and index.
ISBN 1-4042-0072-X (library binding)
1. Cells— Juvenile literature. [1. Cells.]
I. Title. II. Series.
QH582.5.S486 2004
571.6—dc22

                                                    2003021816

Manufactured in the United States of America

Cover: A detail of a microscope

Cover inset: A multi-celled human embryo

Contents

The Cell

The cell can be called the basic unit of life, the building block that makes up every living thing. By studying cells and their construction and interaction with other cells, scientists can learn more about how human, animal, and plant bodies operate, how to better treat illnesses, and possibly even how to correct problems before they occur.

But since most cells are far too small to be seen with the naked eye, no one even knew that such things as cells existed until the invention of the microscope in the sixteenth century. The word "microscope," in fact, comes from the Latin word *microscopium*, meaning "scoping" or seeing things that are "micro" or very small.

TYPES OF CELLS

There are five types of living beings, including animals and plants, all made of cells. Some of these organisms, such as bacteria, are called unicellular (single-celled) creatures. They are literally made up of only one cell. Humans, most animals, and most plants are called multicellular (many-celled) organisms, since they are made up of many cells. The average human body, for instance, is made up of between 10 to 50 trillion cells, and that number is constantly fluctuating.

Cells come in an amazing number of different shapes, depending on what jobs they need to perform. They can look like spirals, balls, rods, coils, or boxes,

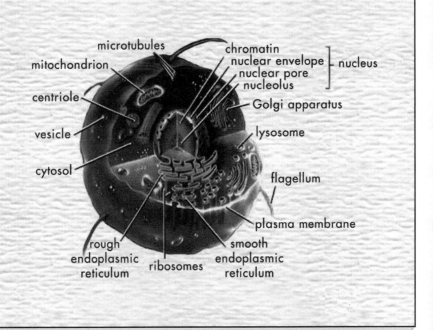

microtubules
mitochondrion
centriole
vesicle
cytosol
chromatin
nuclear envelope
nuclear pore
nucleolus
nucleus
Golgi apparatus
lysosome
flagellum
plasma membrane
rough endoplasmic reticulum
ribosomes
smooth endoplasmic reticulum

This cross section of the cell shows all the different parts that make up the basic building block of all living things. Each part works in harmony with the others to keep the organism alive.

and they can even be shapeless masses. The amoeba, used in so many science fiction and horror movies, is an example of a shapeless yet quite alive unicellular creature. Muscle cells are often long and thin. Nerve cells may look like trees with many branches. There's a reason for each shape. Those long, thin muscle cells, for instance, can more easily contract to do work, while the

many branches of the nerve cells can more efficiently get messages throughout the body.

THE LIFE OF THE CELL

Cells also come in many different sizes. The average cell is about one thousandth of an inch in diameter. The smallest cells, which are certain types of bacteria cells, are about 50,000 times smaller than that. The largest type of cell is one that can actually be seen by the naked eye. This is the yolk of a bird's egg. The largest cell of all is the yolk of an ostrich's egg. But the size of an organism, such as a human being, depends on the total number of cells, not the size of each cell. Each cell, no matter what it looks like, whether it is part of an insect or a human body, is a living thing in itself. It takes in nourishment, gets rid of wastes, matures, reproduces, and eventually dies. It performs all the functions that define a living organism.

Cells reproduce by dividing. When a cell becomes adult, or fully grown, it can divide into two new cells. This form of cell division is called mitosis. First, in a process called nuclear division, the cell's nucleus divides. The chromosomes in the nucleus replicate themselves and double their number. In the second process, called cytokinesis, the cytoplasm divides, and the cell splits itself in half. Each of the two newly produced cells has a complete copy of the original cell's genetic material, its blueprint for making more cells. This is known as asexual reproduction.

There is a second form of cell division, known as meiosis. This is the process of cell division that occurs before a new living being is formed from the merging of a sperm cell and an egg cell. In the process of meiosis, when the nucleus divides, the chromosomes do not double in number. Only half the number of chromosomes from the parent cell goes into each daughter cell. The full complement of chromosomes is restored only when a sperm and egg cell merge. This is known as sexual reproduction.

Each day, several billion cells die in every large, complex living creature. These dead cells either flake off the skin or pass out of the body with other waste. Yet

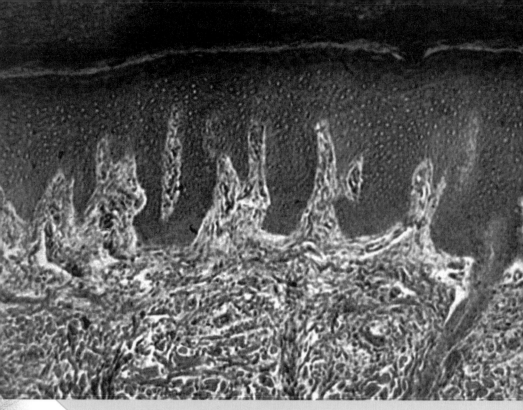

The uppermost cells of a human fingertip are shown here. Dead cells typically make up the thick exterior layer of skin.

the body doesn't start falling apart, nor does it get smaller because of the loss of dead cells. Those dead cells are replaced every day by the same number of new cells through the process of cell division. Some cells, such as white blood cells, are relatively short-lived, with a life span of only about two weeks. The longest living cells are nerve cells, which can last about 100 years, or at least until the body dies.

PARTS OF THE CELL

A cell is an extremely busy organism. It carries out a body's life functions, including growth and reproduction. In addition, all the cells in complex multicellular organisms are specialized and perform different functions. To live and to do its work, a cell must obtain energy. It also must manufacture proteins and all the other substances that are needed for the construction and maintenance of its parts. This requires thousands of chemical reactions. Most of the energy within an animal cell is produced by the mitochondria, tiny rodlike structures within the cell's cytoplasm. The mitochondria are considered the cell's power plants. They take in fuel from the food that was eaten by the body—mostly sugars— and "burn" it with the aid of oxygen molecules to produce the cell's energy. What they actually do is break apart the sugar molecules, a process that releases heat, and this heat is used to induce other chemical reactions in the cell and keep it alive. A cell may contain hundreds or even thousands of mitochondria. Molecules

called enzymes keep chemical reactions within the cell happening at just the right speed.

The cells in plants work slightly differently. Plant cells take in the energy they need directly from the sun in a process called photosynthesis. Molecules of chlorophyll inside the plant cell, located in sacks called chloroplasts, use the light energy of the sun to convert carbon dioxide and water into the sugars that will then be broken apart to create energy. The photosynthetic process cannot produce as much energy as the oxygen-burning process in animal cells, which is one reason why plants cannot perform many of the energy-intensive activities of animals, such as motion and rapid reproduction.

All cells have three main parts, the nucleus, the cytoplasm, and the cell membrane. The cell membrane holds the cell together and controls and regulates what enters and leaves the cell. It is the skin of a cell. Within the cell membrane is the cell's cytoplasm. Within that lies the nucleus, which is the heart of the cell where the genetic material for reproduction is found. There are other structures to be found within the cell's cytoplasm, and these are known as organelles. Mitochondria are organelles. Vacuoles may store nutrients, waste products, or water. A cell is more than 90 percent water. The word "vacuole" comes from the Latin *vacuus*, which means "empty." In some plant cells, a single vacuole can take up most of the space in a cell's cytoplasm.

Another organelle is the lysosome. Lysosomes are round bodies that contain enzymes that can break down many substances. For example, lysosomes inside white blood cells can destroy harmful bacteria. The Golgi apparatus (or complex) is a network of stacked membranes that modifies chemicals so that the cell can use them. It is named after its discoverer, Camillo Golgi. Last, there is the endoplasmic reticulum. This complex network of membranes forms a system of pouches, which store proteins and help channel substances between cells and to various parts of the cell.

The nucleus of each cell is enclosed within a nuclear membrane. Like the cell membrane, this holds

the nucleus together and controls what enters and leaves. Within the nucleus are two important types of structures, the chromosomes and the nucleoli. Chromosomes are thin strands of DNA (deoxyribonucleic acid). The arrangement of molecules along the strands of DNA comprises the genes, the instructions for building more cells. Nucleoli form in certain parts of some chromosomes. Nucleoli help in the formation of ribosomes. Ribosomes are particles of RNA (ribonucleic acid), related to DNA, that are active in creating the body's necessary proteins.

Plant cells also have cell walls, which lie outside the cell membranes and which are made of a substance called cellulose. The fibers of grass and the bark of trees are cellulose. Cellulose cell walls are rigid and give plant cells support but prevent the kind of mobility found in animal cells.

The smallest living organisms, such as bacteria, are made of a single cell. They are called prokaryotic cells, and they are much less complex than other cells. They don't even have a nucleus. This gives them their

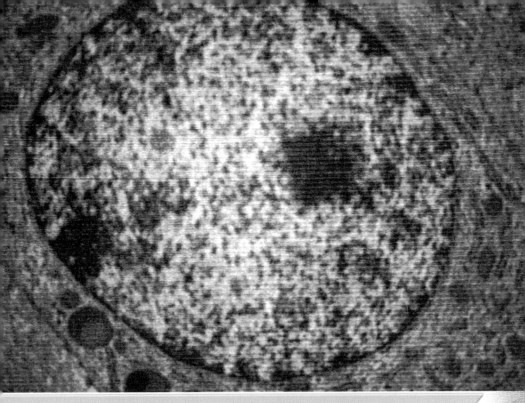

This is a microscopic view of the nucleus of a cell from a complex organism. The dark area (upper right) *is the nucleolus, where ribosomal subunits are assembled.*

name. "Prokaryotic" means "before the nucleus." Cells with a nucleus are called eukaryotic, which means "having a true nucleus."

In multicellular organisms, specialized cells work together to perform a particular job and make up a particular type of tissue, which form an organ, like a heart, stomach, or gland. Examples of specialized cells

are the erythrocytes, or red blood cells, which are highly flexible so they can slip through the smallest blood vessels in a body. These are the cells that make blood red and that carry oxygen and organic substances throughout the body.

When scientists want to study cells, they often culture them. This means growing cells in a special dish. Some cells can't be cultured, but others will readily grow in a dish when surrounded by the right chemical nutrients, and they will even form tissues in a dish. Culturing cells makes it easier for scientists to study them and to perform tasks like testing medicines before trying them on animals or humans.

2

Early Views of the Structure of Life

The story of the cell's discovery is one that is closely linked to the invention of scientific technology. Before something as small as a cell could be seen, the microscope had to be invented. Before the microscope could be invented, glass technology had to be improved. Before that could happen, there had to be the discovery that magnification of images was possible.

OBSERVATIONS OF ANCIENT THINKERS

While there were observant scientists and doctors in the ancient world, there was almost no magnification technology available to them. Even magnifying glasses were unknown before the first century BC. For example, an Egyptian physician in 1600 BC might understand that a particular sickness was caused by unclean water, but he wouldn't know why, whether there were tiny disease-causing animals in the water or if evil spirits were to blame.

The scientists working before the first century BC left little written evidence that they even had theories about the nature of life or its component parts. The earliest clues of what scientists in the ancient world might have thought about living organisms come

Hesire of ancient Egypt's third dynasty was considered a great chief of physicians and dentists. This wood panel is one of the six remaining from his tomb.

from writings from ancient Greece. The Greek philosopher Anaximander, who was born around 610 BC and died in 546 BC, is one of the earliest philosophers of whom we have any record. In addition to being an astronomer, he may have been one of the earliest thinkers to come up with the idea of evolution.

Medieval Muslim physicians believed that a Ruh, *or life force, from a higher force mixed with the anatomic and physiological body to make a complete human being.*

He theorized that some sea creatures had been forced to come ashore, where they evolved into land creatures. But there is no proof that he had any theories about how this might have happened.

Democritus, who was born around 460 BC and died in 370 BC, was another Greek philosopher. While he never actually discovered cells, he did theorize about tiny particles that he called atoms. He said, quite accurately, that atoms made up the entire physical world. He called them *atomos*, which means "indivisible" in Greek, because Democritus defined atoms as the smallest particles of a substance that still had the properties of that substance. It was the beginning of the idea that larger bodies are built up from large numbers of smaller bodies. But, of course, the Greeks were speculating on the basis of logic, which could carry them only so far.

The Greek philosopher Aristotle, who was born in 384 BC and died in 322 BC, was one of the first to base his ideas about the world on the observation of nature. He was particularly interested in trying to classify all animals. While Aristotle had no way of knowing about cells, he did seem to have some concept of their existence and of genetic material as well. He stated:

A given germ does not give rise to any random living being, nor spring from any chance one . . . but each germ springs from a definite parent and

gives rise to a predictable progeny . . . [I]t is the germ that is the ruling influence and fabricator of the offspring."

Aristotle was trying to explain why children resembled their parents, and he used the idea of traits being passed on inside some kind of germ cell during reproduction.

THE FIRST EFFORTS IN MAGNIFICATION

The first discovery of the principle of magnification occurred shortly after these early Greek philosophers. Whoever it was who made the discovery would have probably examined a natural piece of clear crystal that happened to be thicker in the middle than at the edges. This shape is called convex; the opposite shape, with the edges thicker than the middle, is called concave. A modern eyeglass lens is concave, and a modern magnifying glass lens is convex. A convex crystal would make objects look larger and closer than they actually were.

In his thirty-seven-volume Natural History, *Pliny the Elder attempted to describe everything in the natural world.*

In the first century AD, the Roman philosopher Pliny the Elder, who was born in Rome in AD 23 and died in AD 79, and the playwright Seneca, who was born in Spain in 4 BC and died in Rome in AD 65, both mentioned such "magnifying glasses." In fact, Seneca, who was apparently nearsighted, is supposed to have claimed that he read "all the books in Rome" with the aid of a magnifying device made out of a glass globe of water. Pliny the Elder, incidentally, holds the record for being the first scientist to die on a field expedition: He got too close to the eruption of Mount Vesuvius, which destroyed the cities of Pompeii and Herculaneum in AD 79, and

was overcome by toxic volcanic fumes. Seneca fell afoul of politics. His sarcastic works angered Emperor Nero, ruler of Rome, and Seneca was forced to commit suicide. Nero, too, it is said, had poor vision and may even have used a large emerald crystal as a magnifying glass.

Approximately a thousand years after the time of Pliny, improvements in glassblowing and grinding allowed Christian monks in medieval Europe to make use of what they called "reading stones." A reading stone was actually not stone but a sort of magnifying glass. It was sheets of glass, not very well blown but with some magnification properties that allowed the monks to slightly enlarge the figures on a manuscript page as they inscribed them.

By the late thirteenth century in Italy, documents were beginning to mention spectacles, or reading glasses, although no one knows who actually invented the first pair of spectacles. The ground, shaped, and polished glass within the frame that held the spectacles together were called lenses, since people thought they looked a little like lentils. Neither glassblowing nor lens grinding had been truly perfected, however. This meant that lenses weren't very smooth. They might have bubbles in the glass, poorly polished surfaces, or variations in thickness. What's more, there were no such things as optically measured prescriptions. The best that someone in the thirteenth century could hope to get were spectacles that at least cleared his or her blurred vision a little bit.

THE JANSSEN MICROSCOPE

The situation did not change very much through the fourteenth and fifteenth centuries. Then, around 1590, the world of science began to change. Two Dutch makers of spectacles, the father and son team of Hans and Zacharias Janssen, began experimenting with several lenses of different widths and curvatures. They discovered that if they put two nearly identical lenses into two tubes, one that slid into another, nearby objects appeared not merely magnified but greatly enlarged. This discovery led Zacharias Janssen to invent what

may be the first microscope, probably with his father's help since he was still in his teens in 1595. The microscope he built was made up of two convex lenses and three sliding drawtubes, one within another, like the parts of a modern telescope. The microscope was hand-held and could be focused by sliding the drawtubes out or in, increasing or shortening the focal length. The focal length is the distance between the primary lens and the point where the image comes into focus. In general, the longer the focal length, the greater the magnification but the smaller the field of view.

The Janssen microscope could magnify objects up to ten times their normal size, which is not that powerful by today's standards. The fact that it was handheld meant that it could not be kept perfectly still while observing specimens under the lens. But it was important as the ancestor both of the modern microscope and the telescope.

For about fifty years after the Janssen microscope, there were few advances in the science of microscopy. Once again, the problem was the inadequacy of the available technology. The smaller an object, the less light it reflects, and the more light is needed to see it. Janssen lived almost 300 years before the discovery of electricity. Candles did not provide steady enough or strong enough light for accurate viewing. The resolution, or sharpness of the image, seen through early microscopes was also limited by the quality of the available glass for lenses and the imperfections of glassblowing. Even the best glass was not truly clear or well shaped. As a result of these difficulties, few people thought the new invention would ever be of much importance. Since the devices seemed to be useful only for close-up looks at small insects, such as fleas, the popular name for microscopes became "flea glasses."

THE MICROSCOPIC WORLD REVEALED

But glassblowing technology and the new study of optics, the science of light and vision, began to improve by the seventeenth century. Several scientists began to

see the potential of microscopes as more than mere toys. Three of these scientists, one in Italy, one in the Netherlands, and one in England, were contemporaries and belonged to the same scientific society. They even exchanged data with each other.

The Italian scientist was named Marcello Malpighi, and he was born in 1628 and died in 1694. He attended the University of Bologna, intending to become a philosopher. But when Malpighi lost both his parents during his last year in school, he was forced to leave the university to take care of his younger brothers and sisters. Malpighi knew that he needed a career that would make money, and as soon as his parents' debts were paid off, the young man began studying medicine.

It was the right choice. Not only did Malpighi earn his doctorate in both medicine and philosophy, but he seems to have enjoyed his new career, and he became a distinguished professor and physiologist. Physiology is the study of the biological functions of living organisms. Malpighi quickly saw the potential of the microscope, and he used it in much of his research. He did not design

Marcello Malpighi published Anatomia plantarum *in 1679, in which he described the inner structure of roots, stomata, and the fibers of wood in sap.*

his own microscope, but his probably looked something like those being used in Italy at that time: a wooden tube set in a tripod frame to hold the lenses steady.

Malpighi sent his findings to the Royal Society, the English national academy of science that still exists today. It was brand-new in Malpighi's time, having been founded in 1660, and he was one of the first international contributors. His first contribution, in 1661, revealed one of his most important discoveries, made with the help of a microscope. While studying some dissected lung tissue taken from a frog, Malpighi discovered a network of tiny, thin-walled tubes. He named these capillaries, from the Latin

word for "hair," *capillus*. We still use the word today. Malpighi also used the microscope on human tissues. One of the layers of skin he discovered is still called the *rete Malpighi* in his honor. In addition, he also performed the first good comparative study of the liver. Malpighi was also the first to properly describe the formation of the chick in the egg. His microscopic study of plants led to the publication of his *Anatomia plantarum (Plant Anatomy)*. This was a massive book that included many descriptions and his discovery of stomata, which are the pores of leaves.

The Dutch contemporary of Malpighi was Antoni van Leeuwenhoek, who was born in Delft, the Netherlands, in 1632 and who died in 1723. Unlike Malpighi, Leeuwenhoek was not professionally trained as a scientist. In fact, his father made baskets and his mother came from a family of brewers. As a boy, Leeuwenhoek was apprenticed to a fabric merchant, and no one really expected anything more from him than a working knowledge of textiles and salesmanship. Working in the fabric shop may have

Dutch naturalist Antoni van Leeuwenhoek wrote more than 200 letters to the Royal Society of London. The correspondence began when an esteemed physician from Delft, Holland, informed the elite society of Leeuwenhoek's discoveries.

been where Leeuwenhoek first became interested in microscopy. In the fabric shops in his time, magnifying glasses were often needed so that the threads in a piece of cloth could be counted. The idea of counting threads can still be seen in any store selling sheets. Listings for sheets with 180, 200, or more threads per inch can be found.

In Leeuwenhoek's case, his experiments might simply have started as an attempt to design a better magnifying glass. But whatever his inspiration was, Leeuwenhoek did figure out new methods for lens grinding. He eventually began designing his own microscopes, which had magnifications of almost 270 times—a far greater magnification than anything that had ever been seen before.

Around 1654, Leeuwenhoek set himself up in business as a fabric merchant in Delft. He also worked as a surveyor, a wine assayer, and a city official. But Leeuwenhoek also made some of the most important discoveries in the history of biology. He was the first to observe the single-celled microscopic organisms we call protozoa. He observed the fine cellular structure of tissues. He discovered various types of specialized cells, such as blood cells and sperm cells. No one had ever seen such wonders before. Leeuwenhoek discovered the world of microorganisms, living creatures too small to be seen with the unaided eye, and he began to accumulate

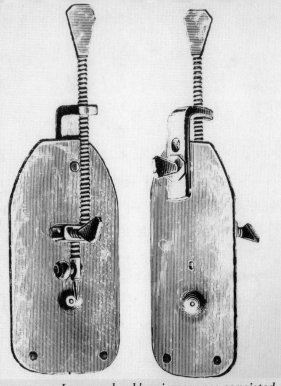

Leeuwenhoek's microscopes consisted of a single lens on a brass plate. The specimen would be mounted on the sharp point in front of the lens.

evidence that the cell was the basic building block of more complex and larger creatures.

Leeuwenhoek also continued to build and refine his own microscopes—some accounts say that he built more than 400, others state that there were more than 500 of them in all. These ranged from very simple designs to others that, because of his skill in lens grinding and polishing, provided the clearest and brightest images available. His microscopes were all very small and similar in design. They were all about 2 inches (5 centimeters) long and 1 inch (2.5 cm) across, were made of metal, and included Leeuwenhoek's excellent glass lenses.

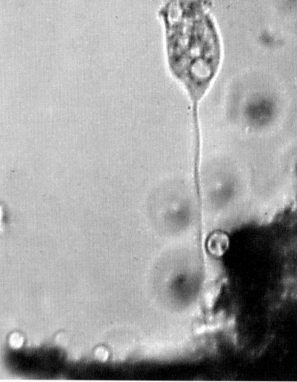

In 1673, Leeuwenhoek began writing letters to the Royal Society in London, describing what he had seen with his microscopes. He continued this correspondence for the next fifty years, and Leeuwenhoek soon became famous in the scientific community. In

Among the protists observed and described by Leeuwenhoek was the ciliate pictured here, Vorticella, *the most complex of the single-celled organisms.*

1680, he was elected a full member of the Royal Society, although he never attended a meeting. Instead of traveling, which doesn't seem to have been something he enjoyed doing, he invited visitors to come to Holland and see the strange things he was describing. He continued his scientific observations until his death.

EARLY VIEWS OF THE STRUCTURE OF LIFE

In a letter written to the Royal Society on June 12, 1716, Leeuwenhoek summed up his life and work, saying that he had followed his work

> not . . . to gain the praise I now enjoy, but chiefly from a craving after knowledge, which I notice resides in me more than in most other men. And therewithal, whenever I found out anything remarkable, I have thought it my duty to put down my discovery on paper, so that all ingenious people might be informed thereof.

A contemporary of both Malpighi's and Leeuwenhoek's, and another important figure in microscopy, Englishman Robert Hooke was born in 1635 and died in 1703. The son of a churchman, the young Hooke was educated at home by his father, although he also served an apprenticeship to an artist that would later prove very useful to him. At the age of thirteen, Hooke went to Westminster School, and after

graduation he went on to Oxford University. It was a time when some of the best scientists in England were teaching and working at Oxford, and it must have been an exciting place for a budding scientist like Hooke. He soon became an assistant to an important chemist of the period, Robert Boyle.

By 1662, Hooke had shown plenty of examples of both his intelligence and his gift for scientific research. He was named curator of experiments of the Royal Society, where he was responsible for demonstrating new experiments at the society's weekly meetings. He later became Gresham Professor of Geometry at Gresham College, London, and lived in London for the rest of his life. Hooke has been called the greatest experimental scientist of the seventeenth century. He was interested in almost every branch of science, including astronomy, chemistry, geology, and physics. Hooke invented the anchor escapement and the balance spring, which made more accurate clocks possible. He served as chief surveyor, helping to rebuild London after the Great Fire of 1666. Hooke also

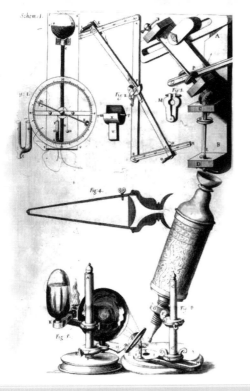

Robert Hooke included this illustration of *the plans for his lens-grinding machine* (above) *and his set up microscope* (below) *in* Micrographia.

worked out the correct theory of combustion, devised an equation describing elasticity that is still used today and is known as Hooke's law, and made important contributions to paleontology and biology.

The importance of Hooke's contributions to biology can be gleaned from his book, *Micrographia*, which was published in 1665. In it, he recorded the scientific observations he'd made with the compound microscope and a new lighting system he'd invented. The compound microscope was a more complex instrument than the simple microscope used by Hooke's Dutch contemporary, Antoni van Leeuwenhoek, with whom he corresponded. This type

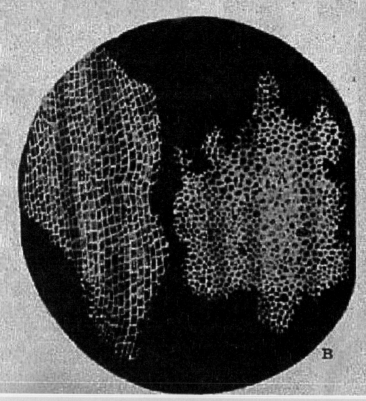

Above is Robert Hooke's representation of cork cells, an illustration included in Micrographia. *The tiny chambers making up the cork reminded Hooke of the "cells" of a monastery, which is how he coined the term.*

of microscope is called compound because it used more than one set of lenses, "compounding," or heightening, the magnification. Although Hooke did not make his own microscopes, he did design them. The microscopes were actually made by the London instrument maker Christopher Cock.

EARLY VIEWS OF THE STRUCTURE OF LIFE

The Hooke microscope had an eyecup, a device that cushioned the face around the eye socket when the user was looking through it. This made it easier to keep the right distance between the eye and the eyepiece. Hooke's microscope had separate drawtubes to provide better focusing and a ball-and-socket joint so that a user could change the angle of the microscope. The tube of the microscope was made of wood covered in leather. With the drawtubes closed, the microscope measured 6 inches (15 cm) long. Unfortunately, the focusing mechanism of Hooke's microscope was not very well designed, and the lens quality could not match that of the simpler Leeuwenhoek microscopes. Hooke, however, preferred his design, claiming that Leeuwenhoek's design, which he had tried, gave him headaches.

Among the subjects that Hooke studied were insects, microscopic animals, and plants. He used his early training as an artist to make detailed and accurate drawings of what he'd seen, and those drawings went into *Micrographia* as well. A perfectly drawn reproduction of an ant takes up one entire page and

This is the library at Magdalene College in Cambridge, England, where the famous diary of Samuel Pepys, along with 3,000 other books and manuscripts, is still preserved.

looks as accurate as any photograph. A new world of microscopic creatures and complex structures was revealed. One of those who really enjoyed Hooke's book was a government official and diarist, Samuel Pepys, who is famous for having recorded a first-person account of the 1666 London fire. Pepys called *Micrographia* "the most ingenious book that I ever read in my life."

Samuel Pepys wrote detailed observations of people and daily life in seventeenth-century London in his famous diaries. Eye strain forced him to quit after nine years.

But the most important contribution Hooke made to biology probably came from his observation of thin slices of cork. Cork is the lightweight, elastic outer bark of the cork oak tree. In "Observation XVIII" of *Micrographia,* Hooke wrote:

I could . . . perceive it to be . . . perforated and porous . . . like a Honey-comb, but . . . the pores of it were not regular . . . these pores, or cells . . . were indeed the first microscopical pores I ever saw.

Not only had Hooke discovered plant cells, he was the first to use the name "cells" for these structures.

He later discovered that other plants had cells as well and that, indeed, all plants he could see through his microscopes seemed to have cells.

But there was a limit to what Hooke could see, even with his compound microscopes. As a result, he never made the discovery that all living things are made up of cells. That discovery would be made in the centuries to come, when more advanced microscope technology became available.

The Eighteenth and Nineteenth Centuries

3

The eighteenth century saw a surge of interest in microscopes, not so much by scientists as by manufacturers. Just about every instrument maker seemed determined to make a better microscope. No fewer than seventy-two variations were produced in the first half of the eighteenth

century. Of these, the most popular was probably that designed by the English instrument maker Edmund Culpeper in the 1720s. The basic Culpeper design had a double set of brass tripods that held the microscope body on its base. Sliding the body in and out of its support tube focused the microscope. Culpeper's instruments were inexpensive, but they lacked an accurate means of focusing. This remained a problem with all microscopes made throughout the eighteenth century.

Despite these problems with focusing, Dutch instrument maker Johan Joosten van Musschenbroek did design a sophisticated, high-power brass microscope with an adjustable fine focus. Van Musschenbroek's microscope was different from the others of its era because its specimen holder was a

Edmund Culpeper's microscope had a concave mirror at its base that reflected light. In this picture, Culpeper's trade card can be seen on the back panel of the microscope's wooden case.

brass plate attached by two screws and a hinge to a brass stem. This design allowed one of the screw adjustments to change the distance between the plate and the stem, while the other screw moved the plate sideways in front of the single lens. Like many of the microscopes developed early in the 1700s, the van Musschenbroek microscope focused on a specimen by moving it back and forth in front of a fixed lens. But this one was more precise because it used the two screws to focus the specimen. Van Musschenbroek's design set a basic standard for many high-power microscopes to follow.

DISCOVERIES ABOUT THE CELL

While the mechanics of the compound microscope were advancing rapidly during this period, there was not a great deal of improvement being made in the field of lens design. Even so, many scientists began to make steady use of microscopes in their work.

THE EIGHTEENTH AND NINETEENTH CENTURIES

Between 1800 and 1840, biologists in particular were using microscopes to study the makeup of plants.

Among the best known of these was the French botanist C. F. Mirabel, who was born in 1776 and died in 1853. He was one of the first to write about plant cells in 1801. The German botanist Kurt Sprengel (1766–1833) was professor of botany at the Halle University and director of the university's botanical gardens. He is noted for his book, *Geschichte der Botanik* (A History of Botany), written in 1817. F. J. F. Meyen (1804–1840) was a professor at the University of Berlin who studied the makeup of plant cells. Scientists were beginning to understand the standardized construction of living organisms from different types of cells.

One nineteenth-century scientist who theorized about cells was Frenchman Jean-Baptiste de Lamarck (1744–1829). Lamarck was a brilliant man who became interested in botany and zoology. His book on the plants of France, *Flore Française,* received a great deal of praise, but didn't earn him much money. He also wrote about

cells, stating in particular that no body could have life if it wasn't made up of cellular tissue. Unfortunately, Lamarck died in poverty and obscurity. He put forward an early theory of evolution, but it proved to be wrong. And he had earned the dislike of two great contemporary scientists, the comparative anatomist Baron Georges Cuvier and the chemist Antoine-Laurent Lavoisier, and these powerful men used their influence against him. All the same, it was Lamarck who popularized the word "biology" and who first drew a distinction between vertebrate and invertebrate creatures (those with and those without a backbone). He did much important work in classifying organisms, drawing a distinction, for example, between the class of six-legged insects and the class of eight-legged arachnids.

Hugo von Mohl (1805–1872) was a professor of botany and dean of mathematics and natural science in Tübingen, Germany. He was considered an expert with the microscope. He even manufactured his own microscope lenses. In 1835, Mohl observed and documented cell division in plant root tips and buds, proving that cells reproduce by division. He also did a great deal of research on the nature of protoplasm. In fact, he was the one who created the word "protoplasm." Hugo von Mohl's works include *Principles of the Anatomy and Physiology of the Vegetable Cell*, published in 1851 and translated into English in 1852, and a collection of important papers, *Vermischte Schriften botanischen Inhalts* (Miscellaneous Botanical Writings) in 1845.

Robert Brown (1773–1858) was a Scottish botanist who was also interested in microscopy. The son of a minister, he studied medicine but worked on his botanical studies between seeing patients. In 1798, Brown happened to meet the eminent botanist Sir Joseph Banks (1743–1820). He was so impressed by him and by the promises of the science that he abandoned a career in medicine for one in botany. Two years later, Brown sailed aboard Banks's ship, the *Investigator,* as chief botanist on a voyage of discovery to Australia. Within three weeks of his arrival in Australia, the eager Brown had collected more than 500 species of plants, almost all of them unknown to Western science. The research

ship returned to England in October 1805 with Brown's drawings and notes, and nearly 4,000 different species of plants. Brown spent five years cataloging the plant samples, which became the core of the plant collection at the British Museum.

British naturalist Sir Joseph Banks traveled around the world with Captain James Cook. His descriptions of the Pacific islands encouraged European settlement there.

Brown made excellent use of microscopes throughout his career, studying both living plants and plant fossils. He was the first person to recognize that every living cell had a heart or a central core, and he gave that core a name: nucleus. He took the word from the Latin word *nucleus*, which means "kernel of a nut." In 1827, he noticed that microscopic particles suspended in liquid tended to move randomly, as a result of collisions with the molecules of the liquid surrounding the particles. The process is now called Brownian motion, and it was important evidence for the existence of atoms.

Johannes Peter Müller (1801–1858) is often described as the father of the German scientific method in medicine. Known for his love of learning and tireless work habits, Müller attended the University of Bonn. He then became a professor of physiology and anatomy in Berlin. Tragically, Müller was known to suffer from depression and anxiety, and his sudden death in 1858 was thought by his associates to have been suicide. While Müller never made any direct discoveries in the field of cellular biology, his greatest impact on the world of science was as a pioneer in scientific thought and the influence he had on his pupils.

One of Müller's students was named Matthias Jacob Schleiden (1804–1881). At first, Schleiden studied not science but law, and in fact he became an attorney. But, like Müller, he suffered from depression, and in

HOW DO WE KNOW
The Nature of the Cell

1832, Schleiden found a gun and attempted to kill himself. He failed, and he wisely decided to change his profession from the one that had made him so desperately unhappy. He found that the world of botany was right for him, although Schleiden continued to fight with bouts of depression for much of his life. Schleiden's work on plant cells led him to announce an important theory. In 1838, he stated that the cell was the basic unit of all plant life. Schleiden's other major contribution to cell biology was his friendship with Carl Zeiss, whom he encouraged to design and build microscopes. The company that Zeiss founded is still a major manufacturer of both microscopes and telescopes.

Another student of Johannes Müller's was Theodor Schwann (1810–1882). In 1836, while still at the University of Berlin, Schwann discovered pepsin. Pepsin is an enzyme that plays a major role in digestion. Schwann had studied microscopic samples of animal tissue and noticed that the samples had nuclear structures similar to those that Schleiden had seen in

Theodor Schwann, the founder of modern histology, coined the term "metabolism" to describe the chemical changes in living tissues.

plants. Working with Schleiden, he expanded Schleiden's original theory by stating that the cell was the basic unit of all plant and animal life.

Schwann and Schleiden realized that some organisms are unicellular while others are multicellular. They also recognized cell membranes, nuclei, and organelles to be common cell features and described them in their comparisons of various animal and plant tissues. These observations and the statement of the cell theory itself were included in Schwann's *Microscopical Researches into the Accordance in the Structure and Growth of Animals and Plants,* published in 1839.

Schwann became a professor at the Belgium Universities in Louvain and Liège. While he was teaching there, he found that yeast was actually a living organism and that sugar and starch fermentation were the result of the yeast cell's life processes. He also studied muscle and nerve structure, and discovered that a coating of special cells, the myelin sheath, protects nerves. Those cells have been named Schwann cells in his honor. He was also the first to realize that an egg is a single cell.

Microscopes continued to improve. A leading Parisian instrument maker named Camille Sebastien Nachet (1799–1881) established the firm of Nachet et Fils in 1839. Nachet was awarded a medal at the Great Exhibition of 1851 for the fine workmanship of his microscopes. He introduced a number of innovations, including the first splitting of the rays in a binocular microscope so that stereoscopic, or dimensional, images could be produced.

Yet another of Johannes Müller's students was Rudolf Carl Virchow (1821–1902). After graduating as a doctor of medicine in 1843, Virchow went on to become one of the most prominent physicians of the nineteenth century, as well as becoming a politician lobbying for improvements in public health.

The prevailing theory of disease in Virchow's time is a strange one by modern standards. In fact, the theory dated back more than 1,000 years and stated that there were four "fluid humors" of the body: hot, cold, moist, and dry. People believed that diseases were caused by an imbalance of the body's fluids: blood, phlegm, yellow bile, and black bile. Virchow put an end to this belief. He proved through his microscopic studies that diseases arose, not in organs or tissues in general, but in individual cells. After studying cell division, Virchow also extended Schleiden and Schwann's cell theory with his statement that *Omnis cellula e cellula,* Latin for "All cells arise from preexisting cells."

Other scientists were making discoveries about the cell as well. One of these scientists was Swiss botanist Karl Wilhelm von Naegeli (1817–1891). Professor at the University of Munich from 1858 until

his death, he was noted for his work on plant cells and plant development. He made studies of the process of cell division in pollen grains and in unicellular algae, and he was the first to figure out the function of many plant parts. In his studies of cells, he made a distinction between the nuclear material and the cytoplasm.

Rudolph Albert von Kolliker (1817–1905), the Swiss anatomist and physiologist, was the author of an influential textbook on cell theory, *Handbuch der Gewebelehre* (The Manual of Histology), which was published in 1852. He also published a text on embryology—which is the study of embryos and how they develop—in which he interpreted the developing embryo in terms of cell theory. In fact, he was one of the first to interpret tissue structure in terms of cellular elements.

By the early 1850s, universities were beginning to offer courses in microscopy. Textbooks, such as the one written by Kolliker and another by Schleiden, were giving students accurate information about cells and cell structure for perhaps the first time in history.

Rudolph Albert von Kolliker was the first to demonstrate how cell division produces the sperm and egg cells from which a new organism is derived.

GENETICS AND THE CELL

One very important discovery, made away from the microscope, was not immediately recognized for its importance. Austrian Gregor Mendel (1822–1884) was a monk, not a scientist. He was very interested in gardening. From 1856 to 1863, Mendel, who was a close observer of nature, raised and analyzed 28,000 pea plants. He studied them to see how such things as color, height, and shape were passed from one generation of plants to the next. He performed similar experiments with several generations of mice, watching

them for size and color. Mendel discovered that there were genetic factors in the parent plants that determined what traits were inherited by the daughter plants. For each pair of traits, one genetic factor appeared to be dominant and the other appeared to be recessive, that is, it did not manifest itself if the dominant factor was present. Knowing this, he was able to predict how many of the offspring would exhibit, for example, a particular height or shape. A flower carrying dominant blue and recessive yellow genetic factors, for example, would always be blue. In 1865, Mendel published his findings. But because he was outside the scientific community, his work went unrecognized until 1900.

Another person whose work went unrecognized until the twentieth century was Swiss biochemist Friedrich Miescher (1844–1895). In 1869, he discovered the nucleic acids within the nucleus of the cell. But no one in the scientific community at the time understood that these substances were the genetic code, so no one saw it as an important or useful discovery.

OPTICAL TECHNOLOGY AND MANUFACTURING

With the second half of the nineteenth century came great improvements in both machine tooling and the field of lens making for microscopes, which would lead to better and more accurate designs for microscopes. Some of the best-known and most successful designers included Beck, Chevalier, Nachet, Leitz, Powell and Lealand, Ross, and Zeiss. Some of these firms are still in business. In fact, Powell and Lealand, as well as Zeiss, still specialize in microscopes and telescopes.

Carl Zeiss (1816–1888) was a famous German instrument maker who founded Carl Zeiss, Inc., which became one of the world's leading manufacturers of optical instruments. He learned about microscopes and other optical equipment while working as an apprentice with Dr. Friedrich Körner, who built microscopes for the German court. Zeiss also studied mathematics, physics, and optics at Jena University. In 1846, Zeiss opened a mechanical

workshop, selling optical and mechanical instruments. Over the next ten years, Zeiss continued to improve the quality and performance of his microscopes and enjoyed continued success. The first Zeiss compound microscope, the Stand One, went on sale in

Carl Zeiss achieved much of his success with microscopes through the process of trial and error. His company still flourishes today.

1857. In 1861, Zeiss was awarded a gold medal at the Thuringian Industrial Exhibition.

By 1866, Zeiss had sold more than 1,000 microscopes. But he was well aware that his own lack of specialized education was keeping him from making more advanced designs. He knew that he needed a more knowledgeable partner. Zeiss found the partner

Manufacturing of large telescopes, such as this one in the Ukraine, led to smaller telescopes, which can be purchased by the general public.

he needed in Ernst Abbe (1840–1905), a brilliant mathematician and physicist who was a professor at the University of Jena. The two men realized that they were interested in solving some of the same optical problems surrounding mid-nineteenth-century microscopy.

Abbe formed a partnership with Zeiss and became the research director of Zeiss Optical Works late in 1866. The two men also became close friends. In 1872, Abbe formulated his wave theory of microscopic imaging and defined what would become known as the Abbe sine condition. This was a mathematical equation that helped researchers improve the

design of microscope lenses. But the glassmaking technology of the era was not up to Abbe's designs. He met glass chemist Otto Schott in 1881, and in 1884, Schott, Abbe, and Zeiss formed a new company known as Schott and Sons in Jena, Germany. In 1886, they introduced the most precise and highest-performance microscope lenses ever built.

When Zeiss died in 1888, Abbe established the Carl Zeiss Foundation in memory of his lost friend. Abbe took control of Zeiss Optical Works and introduced a number of radical ideas to improve working conditions for the employees. These included an eight-hour workday, paid holidays, sick pay, and pensions.

Another optical company, Bausch & Lomb, was founded in the United States by two German immigrants, John J. Bausch (1830–1926) and Henry Lomb (1828–1908). They began by manufacturing a line of eyeglass frames and then expanded into designing reading glasses. From there, they began the production of pocket microscopes, and in 1874, the company produced

Edward Bausch, son of founder John J. Bausch, is pictured here in 1954 holding a microscope he built at the age of fourteen, next to a later model.

its first compound microscope. In that year, the name of the business officially became the Bausch & Lomb Optical Company. By 1900, Bausch & Lomb had become the leading American manufacturer of microscopes and the third largest manufacturer in the world after Ernst Leitz and Carl Zeiss.

STAINING SPECIMENS

Improvements were also being made at this time in the methods of preparing specimens for microscope slides. The use of dyes for staining poorly visible

intracellular structures, such as the nucleus, became more and more common. In 1875, this improved technique allowed German botanist Eduard Strasburger (1844–1912) to observe nuclear division, the splitting of a cell's nucleus.

But even better techniques of specimen preparation and observation came from the Italian doctor and scientist Camillo Golgi (1844–1926). The son of a physician, Golgi studied medicine at the University of Pavia, graduated in 1865, and then worked until 1872 in the Ospedale di San Matteo in Pavia, where he met Giulio Bizzozero, the discoverer of the platelet. Bizzozero introduced Golgi to experimental research and histological techniques, and they became friends for life. Golgi's first publications were on such diseases as pellagra and smallpox. He then began a study of the structure of the nervous system. But financial problems interrupted his academic career in 1872. With the need for a steady income, he accepted the post of chief resident physician in a small hospital near Pavia.

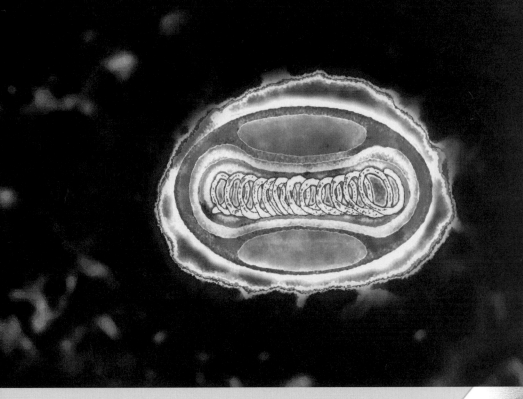

The smallpox virus is made up of one molecule of double-stranded DNA. The deadly virus attaches to the host cell's membrane, then enters the cell and duplicates itself.

Even in this new location, Golgi managed to keep up his experiments and studies. In 1873, working in a makeshift laboratory he'd built in his kitchen, he discovered a method for staining nerve tissue, using the chemical compound silver chromate. Golgi named it *la reazione nera,* or the black reaction. In 1875, Golgi published the first drawings of neural

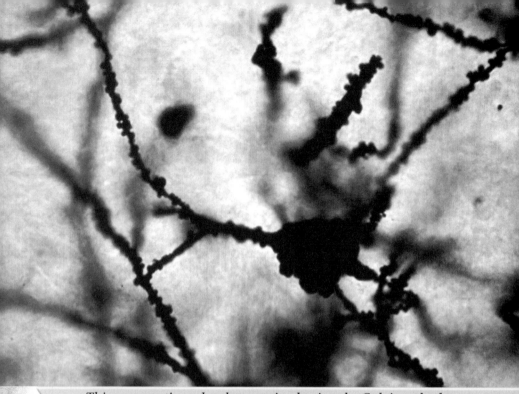

This nervous tissue has been stained using the Golgi method to reveal the parts of the neuron cell. These include the long branches of dendrites that bring information to the cell and extend from the cell body, or soma, as well as the axon, which carries information away.

structures as seen with the help of the technique he had invented. The new staining technique revealed nerve cells in such detail that Golgi was able to confirm the idea that these cells never actually touched but were separated by small gaps called synapses.

In 1880, Golgi described the point now known as Golgi's tendon spindle, and in 1886, he discovered

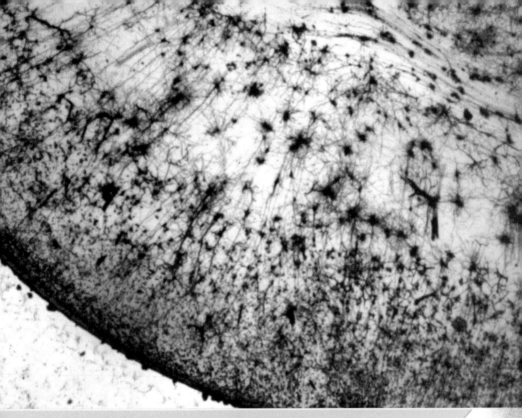

Here, the Golgi staining technique has been used in the cortex, or gray matter of the brain. It is a useful method for indicating any abnormality in the orientation of the neurons.

the presence of nerve cells in an irregular network of fibrils, vesicles, and granules inside the brain, now known as the Golgi apparatus or the Golgi complex. In 1906, after several more years of research into both cells and malaria, Golgi shared the Nobel Prize in Physiology or Medicine with Santiago Ramón y Cajal (1852–1934) for their work on the structure of the

69

nervous system. Golgi became dean of the Faculty of Medicine of the University of Pavia and rector of the university for several years. Golgi also took an active part in public life. He was especially concerned with public health, and he became a senator in 1900. He retired in 1918 but remained as professor emeritus at the University of Pavia.

The Study of
the Cell Today

4

During the early 1900s, Gregor Mendel's work was finally rediscovered by three botanists working separately. Hugo de Vries of the Netherlands, Carl Correns of Germany, and Erich von Tschermak of Austria, each working independently on the problem of heredity, came across

Mendel's findings. In 1902, Walter S. Sutton, an American scientist, pointed out that during cell division, chromosomes did act in a way that confirmed Mendel's ideas of inherited traits. A few years later at Columbia University, Thomas Hunt Morgan (1866–1945) and his associates proved that genes are the units of heredity. They also proved that genes are arranged in a specific order on the chromosomes. All this work was confirmed by Calvin Blackman Bridges (1889–1938), who coauthored an important book, *The Mechanism of Mendelian Heredity*, published in 1915.

ADVANCEMENTS IN MICROSCOPY

Even today, the microscope remains one of the most important tools that scientists use to study cells. Several types of microscopes, including some based on new technologies, are now in regular use.

The first of these microscopes is the optical microscope, also called the light microscope because it

Test tubes placed in a centrifuge are spun at high speeds, using inertia to force the materials in the test tubes to separate.

depends on light waves reflecting off the subject under study. It is the descendant of those used more than 200 years ago by Hooke and Leeuwenhoek. A modern optical microscope can magnify a cell up to 2,000 times. Optical microscopes come in all shapes and sizes. Some of them can be more than 6 feet (1.8 meters) tall.

Modern optical microscopes are often hooked up to computers or video cameras. The main reason why they are still very much in use is that optical microscopes are the only kind that can show living organisms. Once an optical microscope is focused on a specimen, the specimen can be photographed through a technique called photomicrography. The photographs are most often taken through the microscope, although cameras with special lenses can capture images at lower magnifications. For the highest magnification, a camera body is attached to the top of a microscope. The photographer can use colored lighting or a filter to help highlight important details.

Another tool that scientists use to study cells is called the centrifuge. First, the cellular material that researchers want to study is ground up and then placed in a test tube. The tube goes into the centrifuge and is whirled around at a high speed. Centrifugal force separates the ground-up mixture, the heaviest parts sinking to the bottom of the tube and the lighter ones rising to the top. Once the parts have been separated, scientists

74

can study them more accurately. Swedish chemist Theodor Svedberg (1884–1971) won the Nobel Prize for Chemistry in 1926 for his invention of the ultracentrifuge, a more advanced version of the centrifuge.

A special type of optical microscope is the phase contrast microscope, which is often used to examine biological samples. It operates by enhancing the contrasts of light and dark in transparent and colorless objects. The phase contrast microscope can show the components in a cell that would otherwise be very difficult to see. Scientists were first able to watch living cells divide through the use of the phase contrast microscope.

It was the Dutch physicist Frits Zernike (1888–1966) who discovered the principle behind how the phase contrast microscope operates. Although his discovery was made in 1930, it didn't receive much attention until World War II (1939–1945). In 1941, after the German army had invaded and occupied much of Western Europe, including the Netherlands, the Germans took possession of any inventions they felt might be useful to them in the war. The first phase contrast microscopes were manufactured in 1941 for the Germans. After the war, Zernike's achievements were finally recognized, and thousands of phase contrast microscopes were manufactured around the world. He was awarded the Nobel Prize in Physics in 1953.

Above, Fritz Zernike receives the Nobel Prize in Physics. Many living microorganisms can be made easier to see using his phase contrast technique.

Unfortunately, an optical microscope, since it depends on light if the specimen is to be seen, isn't designed to let scientists see objects that are smaller than half the wavelengths of visible light.

Light does, indeed, travel in waves, and the distance between two wave crests or peaks is called the wavelength. But a wavelength of light must be reflected from the object back to the observer to be seen. Details of objects smaller than the wavelengths of visible light cannot be seen in these reflections. Before scientists could see truly tiny particles, they had to use a different form of "light," something with a shorter wavelength.

In 1931, German physicist Ernst Ruska (1906–1988) invented a new form of microscope, the electron microscope. In an electron microscope, electrons, which are subatomic particles, are sent at a high speed through a vacuum to strike a specimen. Modern physics has shown that subatomic particles like electrons also sometimes behave like waves rather than particles and that their wavelengths are much shorter than those of visible light. For this reason, an electron microscope has far better resolution than an optical microscope.

There are two types of electron microscopes. The transmission electron microscope (TEM) produces two-dimensional images, such as images of the details within cells or viral particles, and the scanning electron microscope (SEM) produces three-dimensional images. Instead of the glass lenses focusing the light in an optical microscope, the TEM uses electromagnets to focus the electrons into a very thin beam. The electron beam then travels through the specimen that is being studied. At the bottom of the microscope, the electrons hit a fluorescent screen and create a "shadow image" of the specimen with its different parts displayed in varying degrees of light or darkness according to their density. The images can be studied directly by the operator using a television-type monitor or by photographing them with a camera.

Unfortunately, as mentioned earlier, all electron microscopes have a drawback. Nothing living can survive in their high vacuum, and as a result they cannot be used to study living things. In addition, electron microscopes are very expensive.

UNDERSTANDING THE GENETIC CODE

By the 1940s, scientists had become more and more interested in puzzling out the chemistry of a cell's genes. They already knew that chromosomes consisted of DNA and protein, thanks to the discoveries of Swiss biochemist Friedrich Miescher back in 1869. It wasn't until 1944, however, that a team headed by American geneticist Oswald T. Avery found evidence that DNA actually did determine heredity.

In 1951, George Otto Gey, director of the tissue culture laboratory in the department of surgery at Johns Hopkins Hospital in Baltimore, Maryland, cultivated HeLa, the first established cell line. A cell line is made up of cells of a single type that have been grown in the laboratory for several generations. They are clones of each other and have identical and well-studied genetic material. Comparisons of cell lines yield important information about which genes determine particular features of cells. The name HeLa memorializes the donor of the cells, a young woman named

Henrietta Lacks, who died but whose cells live on. HeLa was used to determine much of what we know about human cells and remains a standard cell for many studies, particularly in the fields of molecular cell biology and genetic disorders.

Scientists already knew that the DNA molecule consisted of specific chemicals: phosphate, adenine, cytosine, guanine, and thymine. But they did not know how these units fit together or how genetic information was encoded in them. In 1953, James D. Watson (1928–), an American, and Francis H. C. Crick of Britain (1916–) proposed that the structure of the DNA molecule resembled a kind of twisted ladder or, more scientifically, a double helix. They based this model on the experimental findings of the British scientists Rosalind E. Franklin (1920–1957) and Maurice H. F. Wilkins (1916–). Franklin had used yet another new technique, X-ray crystallography, to make a photograph of the DNA molecule using X-rays, which also have shorter wavelengths than visible light.

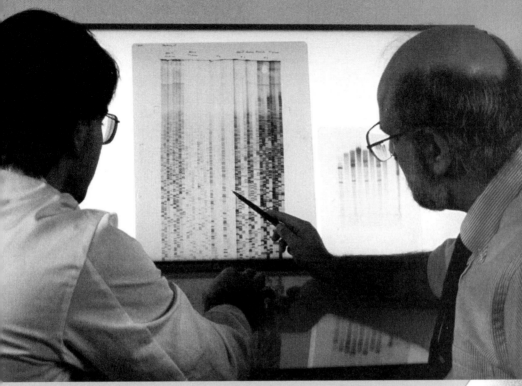

Two scientists examine DNA sequences. Human DNA sequences are more than 99 percent the same across the population, yet slight variations can have a major effect on how individuals respond to disease.

The American biochemist Arthur Kornberg (1918–) was studying the nucleic acids in the cell's nucleus when, in 1957, he was able to produce DNA in a test tube. This accomplishment earned him, together with his fellow researcher Severo Ochoa, the 1959 Nobel Prize for Physiology or Medicine.

American biochemist and molecular biologist Paul Berg (1926–) shared the 1980 Nobel Prize for Chemistry with fellow American Walter Gilbert and Frederick Sanger from the United Kingdom for their studies of the biochemical structure of nucleic acids. Berg's research led him to develop what are now called recombinant DNA techniques, techniques that enabled him to combine parts of the DNA from different species. Experiments with recombinant DNA have helped scientists to learn more about the structure and function of genes and have led to advances in agriculture, medicine, and industry. A new field of the biological sciences known as genetic engineering has arisen as a result of all these discoveries. Once we know which genes are responsible for certain traits in organisms, recombinant DNA technology allows us to remove or replace those genes, giving scientists the power to alter living organisms or create new species.

In 1975, Berg headed an international committee to explore the ethics of genetic engineering and to provide guidelines to regulate genetic research. The proposed guidelines have now been widely accepted. In 1991, he was named chairman of the Program Advisory Committee for the Human Genome Project. This project was meant to map all the genes in human DNA, and it was completed in 2003.

In 1981, Swiss scientist Heinrich Rohrer (1933–) and German scientist Gerd Karl Binnig (1947–) invented the scanning tunneling electron microscope (STM). The STM gives the viewer three-dimensional images of the surface of a specimen. To acquire an image, an extremely fine conducting probe or stylus scans the surface of the specimen. It is so sensitive that it can respond to the voltages generated by electrons in the individual atoms on the surface of an object. By maintaining an even distance from those atoms through very tiny movements of the probe, it can follow even the smallest details of the surface. A profile of the surface is created, and from that a computer-generated contour map of the surface is produced. It is

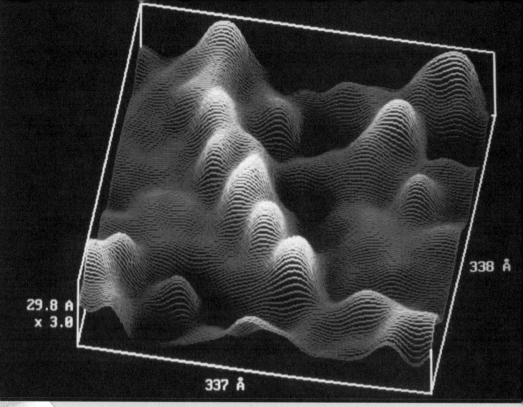

29.8 Å
x 3.0

338 Å

337 Å

This STM image of DNA was taken after an uncoated, double-stranded DNA was dissolved in a salt solution. Scientists hope to sequence DNA by using STM.

also possible to fix organic molecules on a surface and study their structure this way. This technique has been used in the study of DNA molecules. Rohrer and Binnig were awarded the Nobel Prize for Physics in 1986 for their invention.

ALTERING THE CELL'S CODE

In the 1990s, doctors began to use what is now called gene therapy as treatment for certain diseases. This treatment involves inserting a gene into the cells of a patient to correct defects in cell function. The technique holds enormous promise for the elimination of illnesses caused by genetic defects. For example, cells of the pancreas that do not produce enough insulin to prevent diabetes might be altered to work properly. This could improve the health of currently living individuals rather than simply correcting genetic defects in the next generation. The technique is still being improved, and not all the questions surrounding gene therapy have been answered. Will a change to the patient's genome be permanent, or will the patient have to go back to the hospital for "updates" every few months? Will the change affect the rest of the patient's body as well? The effects of genes are fairly complex. It is the job of some genes simply to

turn other genes on or off, so the effects of gene therapy could be far-reaching.

STEM CELLS

One of the newest and most controversial forms of cell research is that concerning stem cells. Most cells within the human body are specialized, with special jobs to do. A cell taken from a muscle, for example, can create only another muscle cell when cloned. But a stem cell is very different. It is an undifferentiated cell found in embryonic tissue that can be made to develop into any of the different cell types that make up the tissues and organs of the body. Some stem cells can also be found in adult organs, but most lines of stem cells are extracted from undeveloped fetuses.

In 1995, Dr. James Thomson and Dr. John Hearn, working at the Wisconsin National Primate Research Center, reported the first isolation and propagation—or growth—of embryonic stem cells. The cells were taken from a rhesus macaque, a species of monkey. The rhesus cells appeared to be capable of differentiating into cells found in bone, muscle, the nervous system, and other tissues. In 1998, using the knowledge they had learned from the rhesus studies, Dr. Thomson and his colleagues isolated and propagated embryo stem cells from humans. As in the rhesus work, the human stem cells were taken from cells shortly after an egg was fertilized and started dividing.

In the years between 1998 and 2003, stem cell experiments have been tried successfully in mice. Heart muscle cells grown from mouse embryonic stem cells have been merged with the heart tissue of a living mouse. This suggests that damaged heart muscles in humans could be repaired with stem cells. In other experiments with mice, damaged spines have been partially repaired with stem cells, suggesting that some day, stem cells will repair spinal injuries. Parkinson's disease may also be curable with stem cells. Successful experiments relating to Parkinson's disease performed on mice took place in September 2003.

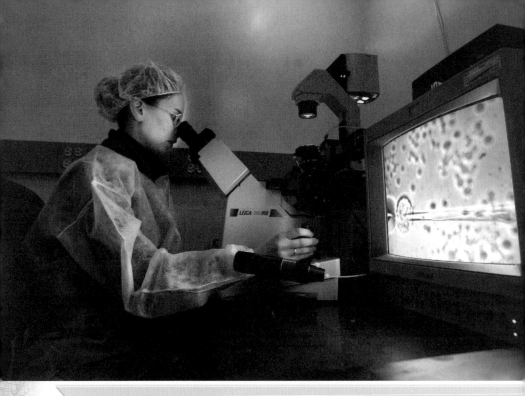

This scientist is injecting mouse embryonic stem cells into a fertilized mouse egg that will then be transferred to a female mouse to give birth. These mice will be used for drug research.

But the use of embryonic stem cells has led to an intense public debate. Is it right to use cells taken from human embryos? Even though the embryos that are used have not yet developed beyond a small ball of cells, some people still think that any embryo is already a human being. But other people believe that the potential medical benefits of stem cells justify their use. Public fears and the government reaction, however, may slow down the study of stem cells.

The use of adult stem cells is seen as a way around these ethical issues. These can be found in many different parts of the human body, from the skin to the brain. Unfortunately, scientists have found problems with adult stem cells that don't arise with embryonic stem cells. First of all, they're more difficult to find amid all the billions of other cells in an adult human. Adult stem cells are also less adaptable and are able to develop only into particular types of cells. However, scientists are working with adult stem cells to see if they can coax the cells to develop in other ways.

On September 23, 2003, Dr. Jose Cibelli and a team of scientists at Michigan State University in East Lansing, Michigan, derived, for the first time, stem cells that are able to develop into many types of cells. Dr. Cibelli and his team did this by harvesting unfertilized eggs from a macaque named Buttercup and using these

Dr. Jose B. Cibelli, pictured here in 2001 when he was vice president of research at Advanced Cell Technology, Inc., first described an experiment cloning human cells in a published paper. In 2004, a Korean team successfully cloned a human embryo and extracted its stem cells.

unfertilized eggs to create parthenotes. A parthenote is an unfertilized egg that has been triggered in a laboratory to divide. Parthenotes that go through only a few cellular divisions may turn out to be a promising source of embryonic stem cells. They seem in every way to be normal, fully functional stem cells. But because no embryo is involved and no human being can possibly grow from an unfertilized egg, some people who are opposed to experiments on embryos may find it easier to accept the use of parthenotes.

Another controversy concerning cellular research is the subject of cloning. Clones are exact duplicates of other living organisms. Clones are actually nothing new. Anyone who has ever grown a plant from a cutting has grown a clone. Most apple trees, for example, are grown from buds cut from trees that have previously produced desirable fruit. The buds are then grafted (attached by placing them into slits cut in plants) to the roots of other trees. The resulting apple trees that grow are clones of the trees from which the buds were cut. Identical twins are also clones.

On February 22, 1997, headlines around the world announced the birth of Dolly, the first cloned sheep. The public was amazed and some people were even frightened. Later in 1997, scientists announced that they had used various cloning techniques to produce other sheep as well as monkeys and calves. By the end of 1997, it seemed to many observers that cloning technology

was on the verge of revolutionizing livestock breeding, drug production, and medical research. But not everyone is happy with the idea. Some people think that cloning is immoral or that it goes against religious beliefs. Just as with stem cell research, public fear may get in the way of science.

But will human beings be cloned for reproduction someday? It's theoretically possible. While cloning humans might be possible, many people fear that human clones will turn out to be monsters, nonhumans, or superhumans. Those who agree with the idea of human cloning say that cloning could give infertile couples, or couples where one person carries a bad gene, a chance for a baby.

But cloning humans may be a much more complicated issue than it seemed at first. An organism may need a complete set of maternal and paternal genes. Scientific evidence indicates that some genes work normally only when inherited from the father and others work normally only when inherited from the mother.

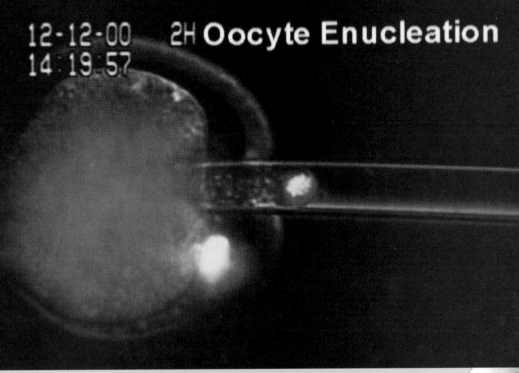

Genetic material is removed from a mammalian egg using suction through a pipette during stem cell research. Experts say it may take years before this science can be applied to actual therapies in fighting human diseases.

There is a growing body of evidence that the genes of clones are not entirely stable and that cloned creatures suffer from many congenital defects and diseases. But if humans can be cloned, what problems would they face? Would a human clone feel that he or she was inferior? Would the parents of a clone value the clone child as highly as they would a "natural" child? And would

cloning lead to efforts to selectively breed children who are healthier and more intelligent?

A clone is not an instant copy of an adult human being. A human clone would still develop as an embryo, then a fetus, and then be born as a baby. It would have its entire life to live as a normal adult, and that person might never encounter the cell donor. The clone would be the equivalent of a delayed identical twin. Identical twins are genetically alike, but they are not the same person because their upbringing and experiences may differ. A clone, growing up decades after the donor of the cell had been born, would experience a different world and different values and as a result would become quite a different person from the cell donor.

THEORIES OF THE CELL'S ORIGIN

One question that is still being asked by scientists but has yet to be answered is: Where did living cells come from? The structures of cells are much more complex

Some scientists believe the first spark of life happened as a result of black iron sulfide released from a deep ocean vent, such as this one located in the Pacific Ocean.

than replicating molecules, so there has to be some interesting history of evolutionary development behind them. How replicating complex molecules appeared is a mystery in itself. Scientists believe that these molecules may have formed either in shallow coastal waters where the energy of the sun was available for reproduction or perhaps near deep vents at the

bottom of the ocean, where energy provided by hot magma (molten rock) was exploited.

As far as cells are concerned, it is possible that some of these complex molecules linked together to form enclosed spheres. Once some of them had done so, they may have had an evolutionary advantage. An enclosed sphere provides a structure with some inherent strength against the stresses of the surrounding environment. Within the sphere, physical processes might have produced a different mix of chemicals from that outside the sphere, a mix of chemicals more suitable to repairing damaged molecules and maintaining the entire structure. Likewise, the nucleus and the organelles, the specialized structures within the cell, may have formed through a similar process of molecular linking, creating spheres within spheres. Or, an intriguing new theory suggests, the first cells may have ingested other smaller cells and adapted them for their own survival. Organelles like chloroplasts and mitochondria may have been primitive bacteria that were absorbed by early cells and put to use to aid their

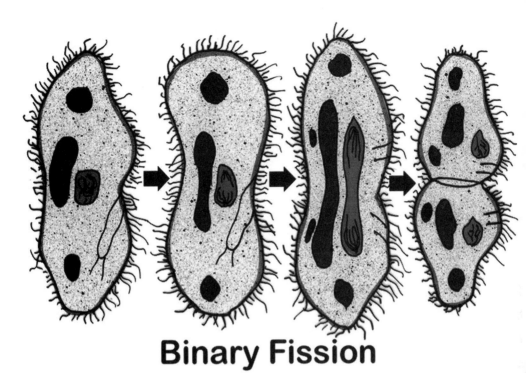

Binary Fission

Binary fission is the reproductive process of prokaryotes, the first form of life on earth, evolving more than 3.5 billion years ago. Prokaryotes do not have an enclosed nucleus, but rather a single chromosome and ribosomes, surrounded by a cell membrane.

survival. Over time, the individual cells themselves came together to form larger and more complex structures that protected each other, and the first primitive multicellular organisms appeared.

There are still many unanswered questions. How did cells acquire the capacity to divide and reproduce themselves (fission)? How did genetic information

become encoded in the complex molecules within the nucleus? How did cells learn to specialize in certain activities and surrender certain survival functions to other cells? Whatever the answers, we can marvel at the wonderful way in which every living organism of every kind has been constructed from these simple building blocks and how these simple structures have modified themselves to produce whatever kind of tissue is required, from nerve cells to heart muscles to the hard exoskeleton of an insect.

No one can say what new discoveries will be made in the study of cells. The future holds enormous challenges and exciting promise for cell research. Although predictions are often wrong, it seems safe to say that some of tomorrow's medical triumphs will probably be in controlling or correcting problems that arise in the cell. Scientists understand how genes manufacture proteins, but many other aspects of how genes operate remain a mystery. Many questions remain to be answered. What causes a cell to die? Can errors in the genetic code that cause mental and physical disorders

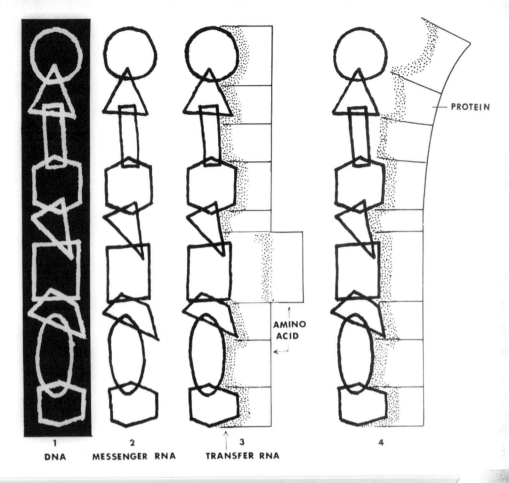

1 DNA	**2** MESSENGER RNA	**3** TRANSFER RNA	**4**

PROTEIN

AMINO
ACID

DNA produces a carbon copy, messenger RNA, which exits the nucleus to provide the information for new tissue. Transfer RNA (shading) chooses amino acids and sequences them to fit messenger RNA, before forming protein, which enables the building of new cells.

be corrected? And most important, are we wise enough to attempt to manipulate the genetic material of living creatures, including ourselves?

If scientists can discover what causes a cell to die, they may be able to slow the aging process and increase the span of human life. As scientists learn more about DNA and the genetic code, they may be able to alter the code and erase hundreds of inherited mental and physical defects. They may learn how to control or cure many forms of cancer. Or perhaps scientists may be able to replace worn-out or diseased tissues. Cloning holds the prospect of growing new organs that would not be rejected by the body's immune system. We are on the verge of discovering some of the deepest secrets of life, and medical science today may seem hopelessly primitive compared to what we may accomplish tomorrow.

Glossary

cell The basic building block of all living things; the smallest unit of self-sustaining living material.

cell division The method by which a single cell divides to create two cells.

clone A line of cells that is genetically identical to the original parent cell.

cytoplasm All the material inside the cell membrane except the nucleus.

differentiation The process whereby an unspecialized early embryonic cell acquires the features of a specialized cell, such as a heart, liver, or muscle cell.

DNA (deoxyribonucleic acid)   A molecule found primarily in the nucleus of cells. DNA carries the instructions for making all the structures and materials the body needs to function.

embryonic stem cells   Undifferentiated cells that have the potential to become a wide variety of specialized cell types.

eukaryotic cells   Cells that have their hereditary material (DNA) in a nucleus that is surrounded by a membrane.

gene   A functional unit of heredity that is a segment of the DNA molecule located in a specific site on a chromosome.

histology   The study of tissues, agglomerations of particular types of cells.

meiosis   The process of division in the nucleus of reproductive cells.

mitochondria A cell's "power plants." They transform chemical energy from food into energy that the cell can use.

mitosis The process of division in the nucleus of a cell.

nucleus The "core" of the cell that contains the cell's genetic material.

RNA (ribonucleic acid) A chemical substance similar to DNA. It carries out DNA's instructions.

stem cells Cells with the ability to divide for indefinite periods in culture and to give rise to specialized cells.

for More Information

ORGANIZATIONS

Centers for Disease Control and Prevention
1600 Clifton Road
Atlanta, GA 30333
(404) 639-3534 or (800) 311-3435
Web site: http://www.cdc.gov/netinfo.htm

World Health Organization
Avenue Appia 20
1211 Geneva 27
Switzerland 41 22 791-3111
e-mail: library@who.int

WEB SITES

Due to the changing nature of Internet links, the Rosen Publishing Group, Inc., has developed an online list of Web sites related to the subject of this book. This site is updated regularly. Please use this link to access the list:

http://www.rosenlinks.com/gsq/nace

For Further Reading

Dobell, C. *Antony van Leeuwenhoek and His "Little Animals."* New York: Dover Publications, 1960.

Ford, Brian J. *Single Lens: The Story of the Simple Microscope.* New York: HarperCollins, 1985.

Harris, H. *The Birth of the Cell.* New Haven, CT: Yale University Press, 1998.

Watson, James D. *The Double Helix: A Personal Account of the Discovery of the Structure of DNA.* New York: Touchstone Books, 2001.

Bibliography

Adelmann, Howard B. *Marcello Malpighi and the Evolution of Embryology*. New York: Cornell University Press, 1966.

Lodish, Harvey, et al. *Molecular Cell Biology*. 4th edition. New York: W. H. Freeman & Co., 1999.

Martin, Gerry. *Glass: A World History*. Chicago: University of Chicago Press, 2002.

Rasmussen, Nicholas. *Picture Control: The Electron Microscope and the Transformation of Biology in America, 1940–1960*. Cambridge, UK: Cambridge University Press, 1999.

Index

Credits

ABOUT THE AUTHOR

Josepha Sherman is a professional author and folklorist, with more than forty books and 125 stories and articles in print. She's an active member of the Author's Guild and the Science Fiction Writers of America. Her web site is at http://www.josephasherman.com.

PHOTO CREDITS

Designer: Evelyn Horovicz; **Editor:** Leigh Ann Cobb;
Photo Researcher: Nelson Sá